Pandas

Katie Franks

PowerKiDS press.

New York

Published in 2015 by The Rosen Publishing Group, Inc.
29 East 21st Street, New York, NY 10010 ·

Copyright © 2015 by The Rosen Publishing Group, Inc.

First Edition

Editor: Jennifer Way
Photo Research: Katie Stryker
Book Design: Joe Carney

Photo Credits: Cover Pete Ryan/National Geographic/Getty Images; pp. 5, 17, 22 Hung Chung Chih/Shutterstock.com; p. 6 katatonia82/Shutterstock.com; p. 9 Tao Jiarong/iStock/Thinkstock; p. 10 Olga Bogatyrenko/Shutterstock.com; pp. 13, 21 Keren Su/The Image Bank/Getty Images; p. 14 Zastolskiy Victor/Shutterstock.com; p. 18 Keren Su/China Span/Getty Images; p. 24 Alexander Mackenzie/iStock/Thinkstock.

Library of Congress Cataloging-in-Publication Data

Franks, Katie.
  Pandas / by Katie Franks. — 1st ed.
     pages cm. — (The zoo's who's who)
Includes index.
  ISBN 978-1-4777-6578-4 (library binding) — ISBN 978-1-4777-6581-4 (pbk.) —
ISBN 978-1-4777-6582-1 (6-pack)
  1. Giant panda—Juvenile literature. I. Title.
  QL737.C27F72 2015
  599.76'3—dc23
                                       2013048504

Manufactured in the United States of America

CPSIA Compliance Information: Batch #WS14PK4: For Further Information contact Rosen Publishing, New York, New York at 1-800-237-9932

Contents

The giant panda lives in China. It is famous for its black and white fur.

Pandas live in forests. These forests are in the mountains in central China.

Pandas eat mostly **bamboo**. They sometimes eat other plants or small animals.

Pandas have special bones in their front **paws**. These bones work like thumbs. These bones help them grab bamboo.

Pandas spend most of their time on the ground. They can **climb** trees, though.

Pandas are part of the bear family. There are eight kinds of bears.

A baby panda is a **cub**.
Mothers care for their cubs for
about two years.

17

Scientists at zoos help pandas have babies. They also help mothers care for their cubs.

Mothers mostly have one cub at a time. Fathers do not raise the cubs. Pandas mostly live alone in the wild.

21

Pandas are rare. Only 1,600 live in the wild. About 300 live in zoos around the world.

WORDS TO KNOW

bamboo

climb

cub

paws

WEBSITES

Due to the changing nature of Internet links, PowerKids Press has developed an online list of websites related to the subject of this book. This site is updated regularly. Please use this link to access the list:
www.powerkidslinks.com/zww/panda/

INDEX